D1035853

Together Forever

THIS IS A PRION BOOK

First published in Great Britain in 2016 by Prion
An imprint of the Carlton Publishing Group
20 Mortimer Street
London W1T 3JW

A CIP catalogue for this book is available from the British Library.

ISBN 978-1-85375-949-9

Printed in Dubai

10 9 8 7 6 5 4 3 2 1

Together Forever

Humorous and Inspirational Quotes
Celebrating Love and Marriage

PRION

Contents

Introduction

Everyone loves a wedding – it is all things in one: a solemn occasion, a reunion, a fashion parade, a party and, above all, a love story. It is one of life's momentous events and of course it has been a focus for wits and sages throughout the years. Writers and comedians, poets, pop stars and politicians have all contributed observations, quips, common sense and pure romantic sentiment.

This book has assembled the wittiest, most pithy and dreamy of these – a perfect selection for those looking forward to their own wedding, couples celebrating their nuptials or anyone who sheds a happy tear at the mere utterance of 'I do'.

Soulmates

"I love you because the
entire universe conspired to
help me find you."

Paolo Coelho

"Finding someone you love
and who loves you back is a
wonderful, wonderful feeling. But
finding a true soul mate is an even
better feeling."

Cecelia Ahern

"Once in a while, right in the middle of an ordinary life, love gives us a fairy tale."

Anon

"What the heart knows today the head will understand tomorrow."

James Stephens

"Me and my wife met at a castanet class. We clicked."

Stewart Francis

"Grief can take care of itself, but to get the full value of joy, you must have somebody to divide it with."

Mark Twain

"The heart wants what it wants. There's no logic to these things. You meet someone and you fall in love and that's that."

Woody Allen

"I know there is strength in the differences between us and I know there is comfort where we overlap."

Ani Difranco

"My wife picked me out of a football sticker book and I chose her from a music video off the television."

David Beckham

"Because she is my friend and my wife, she has seen and brought out the best and worst of me, and she is still with me, and I owe her my whole heart, soul, attention, love and anything she desires of me. She will always be there."

Dagny Connolly

"We have the greatest pre-nuptial agreement in the world. It's called love."

Gene Perret

"I dreamed – and this dream
was the finest – that all I dreamed
was real and true, and we would
live in joy forever, you in me
and me in you."

Clive Barker, Days of Magic, Nights of War

"We are each other's harvest; we are
each other's business; we are each
other's magnitude and bond."

Gwendolyn Brooks

"Life is a game and true
love is a trophy."

Rufus Wainwright

"For true love is inexhaustible; the
more you give, the more you have.
And if you go to draw at the true
fountainhead, the more water you
draw, the more abundant is its flow."

Antoine de Saint-Exupery

"It may be an old cliche, but I think true love will last; it has no end. But finding the right person is a very difficult thing."

Bruce Forsyth

"I love you, not only for what you are, but for what I am when I am with you. I love you not only for what you have made of yourself, but what you are making of me."

Elizabeth Barrett Browning

"Something happened to me.
It was the sweetest thing that
ever could be. It was a fantasy,
a dream come true. It was the day
I met you!"

Mandy Forkner

"Only one is a wanderer; two together
are always going somewhere."

Vertigo

"I dunno, she's got gaps, I got gaps,
together we fill gaps."

Rocky

"Love is a fire that feeds our life."
Pablo Neruda

"You are the finest, loveliest,
tenderest and most beautiful person
I have ever known, and even that
is an understatement."
F. Scott Fitzgerald

"Don't ever think I fell for you,
or fell over you. I didn't fall in
love, I rose in it."
Toni Morrison

"I believe that two people are connected at the heart, and it doesn't matter what you do, or who you are or where you live; there are no boundaries or barriers if two people are destined to be together."

Julia Roberts

"Before we met, I was as lost as a person could be and yet you saw something in me that somehow gave me direction again."

Nights in Rodanthe

"True love doesn't happen right away; it's an ever-growing process. It develops after you've gone through many ups and downs, when you've suffered together, cried together, laughed together."

Ricardo Montalban

"True love is eternal, infinite and always like itself. It is equal and pure, without violent demonstrations: it is seen with white hairs and is always young in the heart."

Honore de Balzac

The Proposal

"As soon as I saw you I knew an adventure was going to happen."

Winnie the Pooh

"When you realise you want to spend the rest of your life with somebody you want the rest of your life to start as soon as possible."

Nora Ephron

"If nothing lasts forever, will you be my nothing?"

Anon

"When my boyfriend proposed marriage to me I said: 'I love the simple things in life, but I don't want one of them for my husband."

Anon

"You have bewitched me body and soul and I love... I love... I love you. And I never wish to be parted from you from this day on."

Mr Darcy, Pride & Prejudice

"Personally, I'm an advocate for short engagements. Long sometimes means there is a reason for it. Two years engaged and no wedding... I'd be upset."

Emily Blunt

"I wanted to marry her ever since I saw the moonlight shining on the barrel of her father's shotgun."

Eddie Albert

"Before getting married, find out if you're really in love. Ask yourself, 'Would I mind getting financially destroyed by this person'?"

Johnny Carson

"As for me, to love you alone, to make you happy, to do nothing which would contradict your wishes, this is my destiny and the meaning of my life."

Napoleon Bonaparte

"Come, let's be a comfortable couple and take care of each other! How glad we shall be, that we have somebody we are fond of always, to talk to and sit with."

Charles Dickens

"I wanted to have a pre-nuptial agreement. Not to get married."

Anne MacHale

"I told my father I had half a mind to get married. He said that was all I needed."

Roy Brown

"The proposal is the only thing that the guy has control over in the entire wedding deal. It is your one chance to make this moment stand out, not only for you, but for her."

Drew Seeley

"In all seriousness, I don't get people who need to make a proposal a bigger deal than marriage already is."

Julie Klausner

"The moment I was introduced to my wife, Emma, at a party I thought, here she is – and 20 minutes later I told her she ought to marry me. She thought I was as mad as a rat. She wouldn't even give me her telephone number – and she wrote in her diary: 'A funny little man asked me to marry him.'"

Julian Fellowes

"I am not married, no. I wasn't really into the notion when I was younger, but now I think a proposal is the ultimate romantic gesture."

Miranda Hart

"To speak frankly, I am not in favour of long engagements. They give people the opportunity of finding out each other's character before marriage, which I think is never advisable."

Oscar Wilde,
The Importance of Being Earnest

"You make me happier than I ever thought I could be, and if you let me I will spend the rest of my life trying to make you feel the same way."

Chandler proposing to Monica, Friends

"Because today, when I look into your eyes, my love for you only grows. It's even stronger now. My love will never waver. And this I vow to you, today, and always and forever."

One Tree Hill

"An engagement in war is a battle.
In love it is the salubrious calm that
precedes the real hostilities."

Gideon Wurdz

"I guarantee that we'll have tough
times. I guarantee that at some
point one or both of us will want
to get out. But I also guarantee
that if I don't ask you to be mine,
I'll regret it for the rest of my life.
Because I know in my heart, you're
the only one for me."

Ike Graham, The Runaway Bride

"Marriage was created not to be
a background but to need one.
Mine is going to be outstanding.
It can't, shan't, be the setting – it's
going to be the performance, and
the world shall be the scenery."

F. Scott Fitzgerald

"How can I choose a husband when
I can't even decide what to wear?"

Beth Jaykus

"I just hoped that... that I'd meet some nice friendly girl, like the look of her, hope the look of me didn't make her physically sick, then pop the question and, um, settle down and be happy. It worked for my parents. Well, apart from the divorce and all that."

Tom, Four Weddings and a Funeral

"Wow! Let's have a look at the engagement ring. It's beautiful. When is the stone being put in?"

Will Truman, Will and Grace

"My fiancé and I are having a little disagreement. What I want is a big church wedding with bridesmaids and flowers and a no-expense spared reception; and what he wants – is to break off our engagement."

Sally Poplin

"You don't marry the person you can live with... you marry the person you can't live without."

Anon

"We are all a little weird and life's a little weird, and when we find someone whose weirdness is compatible with ours, we join up with them and fall in mutual weirdness and call it love."

Robert Fulghum

"She was so sweet that we just walked in the park and I was so touched by her that after 15 minutes I wanted to marry her, and after half an hour I completely gave up the idea of snatching her purse."

Woody Allen

Marriage Is...

"Marriage is a mosaic you build with your spouse. Millions of tiny moments that create your love story."

Jennifer Smith

"Marriage is a series of desperate arguments people feel passionately about."

Katharine Hepburn

"Marriage is getting to have a sleepover with your best friend, every single night of the week."

Christie Cook

"Marriage is being pretty damn sure you could identify your husband in a pitch black room by his farts alone."

Laura Looch

"Marriage is listening to your spouse tell the same joke to different people and trying to act amused every time."

Kathleen Snow

"Marriage is like twirling a baton, turning a handspring or eating with chopsticks; it looks easy until you try it."

Helen Rowland

"Marriage is like pantyhose. It all depends on what you put into it."

Phyllis Schlafly

"Marriage is not a ritual or an end. It is a long, intricate, intimate dance together and nothing matters more than your own sense of balance and your choice of partner."

Amy Bloom

"Marriage is a sort of friendship
recognised by the police."

Robert Louis Stevenson

"Marriage is a ghastly public
confession of a strictly private
intention."

Ian Hay

"Marriage is the most advanced form
of warfare in the modern world."

Malcolm Bradbury

"Marriage is when a woman
asks a man to remove his pyjamas
because she wants to send them
to the laundry."

Albert Finney

"Marriage is like a bank account.
You put it in, you take it out,
you lose interest."

Professor Irwin Corey

"Marriage is like vitamins: we supplement each other's minimum daily requirements."

Kathy Mohnke

"Marriage is a three-ring circus. First the engagement ring, then the wedding ring, then the suffering."

Milton Berle

"Marriage is not just spiritual communion and passionate embraces; marriage is also three-meals-a-day and remembering to carry out the trash."

Joyce Brothers

"Marriage is a lot like the army: everyone complains, but you'd be surprise at the large number that re-enlist."

James Garner

"Marriage is the golden ring in a chain whose beginning is a glance and whose ending is eternity."

Kahlil Gibran

"Marriage is a wonderful institution. If it weren't for marriage, husbands and wives would have to fight with total strangers."

Patrick Murray

"Marriage is natural: like poaching, or drinking or wind in the stummick."

H.G. Wells

"Marriage is an outmoded
silly convention started by the
caveman and encouraged by florists
and the jewellers."

Olivia de Havilland

"Marriage is a very good thing, but
it's a mistake to make a habit of it."

Somerset Maugham

"Marriage is like the Middle East –
there's no solution."

Shirley Valentine

"A marriage is like a long trip in a tiny rowboat; if one passenger starts to rock the boat, the other has to steady it; otherwise they will go to the bottom together."

David Reuben

"Here's to matrimony, the high sea for which no compass has yet been invented."

Heinrich Hesse

"Marriage is a wonderful invention. Then again so is a bicycle repair kit."

Billy Connolly

"Love is blind. Marriage is the eye-opener."

Pauline Thomason

"Marriage is like pi – natural, irrational and very important."

Lisa Hoffman

"Marriage is like putting your hand into a bag of snakes in the hope of pulling out an eel."

Leonardo Da Vinci

"Marriage is like having to stand on one leg for the rest of your life."

Phillip Larkin

"Love is the title while marriage is the whole story."

Anon

"Getting married is a lot like getting
into a tub of hot water. After you
get used to it, it ain't so hot."

Minnie Pearl

"Marriage is a book of which the
first chapter is written in poetry and
the remaining chapters in prose."

Beverley Nichols

"We need a witness to our lives. There's a billion people on the planet... I mean, what does any one life really mean? But in a marriage, you're promising to care about everything. The good things, the bad things, the terrible things, the mundane things... all of it, all of the time, every day. You're saying 'Your life will not go unnoticed because I will notice it. Your life will not go un-witnessed because I will be your witness.'"

Shall We Dance?

"Marriage has no guarantees. If that's what you're looking for, go live with a car battery."

Erma Bombeck

"A good marriage is at least 80% good luck in finding the right person at the right time. The rest is trust."

Nanette Newman

"A good marriage is like a casserole: only those responsible for it really know what goes in it."

Anon

The Wedding Ceremony

"Love is a flower which turns
into fruit at marriage."

Finnish proverb

"Love is the sweetest affection,
dictated by the heart, spoken by the
lips and proven at the altar."

Anon

"The highest happiness on earth
is the happiness of marriage."

William Lyon Phelps

"The real act of marriage takes place in the heart, not in the ballroom or church or synagogue. It's a choice you make on your wedding day, and over and over again, and that choice is reflected in the way you treat your husband."

Barbara De Angelis

"In my wedding... Well, in my wife's wedding that I was allowed to go to..."

Craig Ferguson

"What greater thing is there for two human souls than to feel that they are joined for life... to strengthen each other... to be at one with each other in silent unspeakable memories."

George Eliot

"My friend got a personal trainer a year before his wedding. I thought, 'Bloody hell. How long's the aisle going to be?'"

Paul McCaffrey

"For my wedding I'm trying to get into shape. The shape I picked is a triangle."

Dawn French

"Do you think the night before a Mormon wedding a guy says, 'How am I gonna sleep with the same eight women for the rest of my life?'"

Eric, Entourage

"On the morning of the wedding, she was in a complete panic. She said 'Something old, something new – I've got nothing borrowed and blue!' I said, 'You've got a mortgage and varicose veins, will that do?'"

Victoria Wood

"I can't explain why a bride buys her wedding dress, whereas a groom rents his tux."

Lou Holtz

"My wife spent a fortune on a wedding
dress. Complete waste of money to my
mind. She's worn it once. I've worn it
more than she has."

Mike Gunn

"I couldn't believe the groom
was married in rented shoes. You're
making a commitment for a lifetime
and your shoes have to be back
by 5.30pm."

Jerry Seinfeld

"Since Americans throw rice at weddings, do Asians throw hamburgers?"

Steven Wright

"Two TV aerials meet on a roof, fall in love, get married. The ceremony was rubbish, but the reception was brilliant!"

Tommy Cooper

"I had a fairytale wedding –
Grimm!"

Marti Caine

"My wife and I were married
in a toilet: it was a marriage of
convenience."

Tommy Cooper

"I always cry at weddings,
especially my own."

Humphrey Bogart

"No matter what kind of music you asked them to play, your wedding band play will play it in such a way that it sounds like "New York, New York"."

Dave Barry

"I love DJs at weddings, DJs that talk all night and you can't understand a word they say."

Peter Kay

"Wedding rings: the world's
smallest handcuffs."

Homer Simpson

"They didn't give a wedding list,
but the last thing I got him – he's a
very difficult man to get presents for
– was some coffee from Cambodian
weasel vomit."

*Stephen Fry on his wedding gift to
Charles and Camilla*

"You can't have everything you want on a wedding list. Certain things don't go. Xbox 360 games don't go on a wedding list... They can go on the list, but they'll have mysteriously disappeared... replaced by something called a soup tureen."

Ed Byrne

"Love is a temporary insanity curable by marriage."

Ambrose Bierce

"The most dangerous food is
the wedding cake."

James Thurber

"A wedding invitation is a
beautiful and formal notification
of the desire to share a solemn and
joyous occasion, sent by people who
have been saying, 'Do we have to
ask them?' to people whose first
response is, 'How much to you think
we have to spend on them?'"

Judith Martin

"The groom always smiles proudly because he's convinced he's accomplished something quite wonderful. The bride smiles because she's been able to convince him of it."

Judith McNaught

"You can always spot the father of the bride – he's the one signing his retirement fund to the caterer."

Joe Hickman

"Love is the ultimate outlaw.
It just won't adhere to any rules.
The most any of us can do is to
sign on as its accomplice. Instead
of vowing to honor and obey, maybe
we should swear to aid and abet.
That would mean that security is
out of the question. The words
'make' and 'stay' become
inappropriate. My love for you has no
strings attached. I love you for free."

Tom Robbins

"It's too bad that in most marriage ceremonies they don't use the word 'obey' any more. It used to lend a little humour to the occasion."

Lloyd Cory

"I don't think their marriage will last. When the groom said 'I do', the bride said 'Don't use that tone of voice with me.'"

Gary Apple

"Vol-au-vents, chicken legs, cheesecake... Vol-au-vents, chicken legs, cheesecake... That's all there is. The same food repeated. One table and a shit load of mirrors, that's the wedding buffet."

Peter Kay

"We thought it was a bad idea you guys got married, but we didn't feel like we could say anything because it was an open bar."

Megan Mooney

"A wedding is a sacrament... a joyous celebration of love and commitment. In Utopia. In the real world... it's an excuse to drink excessively and say things you shouldn't say."

Nick Mercer, The Wedding Date

"To look beautiful at your wedding, take time to plan it. It took me a long time to find two ugly bridesmaids and a frumpy little flower girl."

Phyllis Diller

"Barbara: Two hundred pounds.
Denise: How many tiers is that?
Jim: There'll be plenty of bloody
tears if it's two hundred pounds."

The Royle Family

"He made them put about four
or five bottles of brandy in that
cake. Ozzy ate it – he ate the whole
cake – and was laid out... He never
made it into the bedroom on our
wedding night."

Sharon Osbourne

"You'll want to have lots of photographs of your wedding to show your family and friends, who will have been unable to see the actual ceremony because the photographer was always in the way."

Dave Berry

"I'll try to make our lives the best piece of art I've ever done."

Jewel Kilcher

"You sacrificed an hour of good drinking time so he could get some nice angles of you on the swing, under the weeping willow tree in the churchyard. And where's the video now? I bet half of you don't even know."

Jeremy Clarkson

"And we've got a toaster and everything. So there is no reason for the wedding."

Karl Pilkington

"They put these one-time use cameras on the tables. I thought that was a great idea – 'til they got the pictures back, realised only them little bad kids had the cameras. They're going through hundreds of pictures like, 'Oh, here's another one of the cat's butt.'"

Clinton Jackson

"Tom [Cruise] and I will always be in our honeymoon phase."

Katie Holmes

"I dreamed of a wedding of elaborate elegance/A church filled with family and friends/I asked him what kind of a wedding he wished for/He said one that would make me his wife."

Anon

"In Hollywood, brides keep the bouquets and throw away the groom."

Groucho Marx

"To love each other, even when we hate each other. No running ever; nobody walks out no matter what happens. Take care when old, senile, smelly. This is forever."

Meredith and Derek, written on a Post-it note, Grey's Anatomy

"The night of our honeymoon my husband took one look and said, 'Is that all for me?'"

Dolly Parton

As far as I'm concerned, my daughter could not have chosen a more delightful, charming, witty, responsible, wealthy (let's not deny it), well-placed, good-looking, and fertile young man than Martin as her husband. And I therefore ask the question: why the hell did she marry Gerald instead?"

Rowan Atkinson, Wedding from Hell sketch

"A honeymoon is a short period of doting between dating and debting."

Ray Bandy

"Mawage. Mawage is wot bwings us togeder tooday. Mawage, that bwessed awangment, that dweam wifin a dweam... And wuv, tru wuv, will fowow you foweva... So tweasure your wuv."

The Princess Bride

"All honeymooners should hire a third party to ease the conversation during that most difficult time."

Robert Morley

"When I was young it was considered immodest for the bride to do anything on the honeymoon except to weep gently and ask for glasses of water."

Noël Coward

A Little
Advice

"All those 'and they lived happily ever after' fairytale endings need to be changed to '...and then they began the very hard work of making their marriages happy.'"

Linda Miles

"Always get married early in the morning. That way, if it doesn't work out, you haven't wasted a whole day."

Mickey Rooney (married eight times)

"The dedicated life is the life worth living. You must give with your whole heart."

Anne Dillard

"I was married by a judge. I should have asked for a jury."

Groucho Marx

"Gays and lesbians getting married – haven't they suffered enough?"

Michael Shaw

"I think men who have a pierced ear
are better prepared for marriage.
They've experienced pain and
bought jewellery."

Rita Rudner

"We sleep in separate rooms, we
have dinner apart, we take separate
vacations – we're doing everything
we can to keep our marriage
together."

Rodney Dangerfield

"All marriages are happy. It's trying to live together afterwards that causes all the problems."

Shelley Winters

"What's the best way to have your husband remember your anniversary? Get married on his birthday."

Cindy Garner

"Marrying a man is like buying something you've been admiring for a long time in a shop window. You may love it when you get it home, but it doesn't always go with everything else."

Jean Kerr

"Women hope men will change after marriage, but they don't; men hope women won't change, but they do."

Bettina Arndt

"Success in marriage does not
come merely through finding the
right mate, but through being
the right mate."

Barnett Brickner

"Marriage should be a duet –
when one sings, the other claps."

Joe Murray

"What's the difference between
a boyfriend and a husband?
About 30 pounds."

Cindy Garner

"My wife, Mary, and I have been married for 47 years and not once have we had an argument serious enough to consider divorce; murder, yes, but divorce, never."

Jack Benny

"Marriages we regard as the happiest are those in which each of the partners believes he or she got the best of it."

Sydney J. Harris

"The best thing that can happen
to a couple married 50 years
or more is that they both grow
nearsighted."

Linda Fiterman

"Sexiness wears thin after a while,
but to be married to a man who
makes you laugh every day, ah, now
that's a real treat."

Joanne Woodward

"We cannot really love anybody
with whom we never laugh."

Agnes Repplier

"Take each other for better or
worse, but not for granted."

Arlene Dahl

"The great secret of successful
marriage is to treat all disasters
as incidents and none of the
incidents as disasters."

Harold Nicolson

"Never forget the nine most
important words of any marriage:
1. I love you
2. You are beautiful
3. Please forgive me."

H. Jackson Brown, Jr.

"Happy marriages begin when
we marry the ones we love, and
they blossom when we love the
ones we marry."

Tom Mullen

"Tell everyone that when the day is out we shall have a wedding. Or a hanging. Either way, we're gonna have a lot of fun. Huh?"

Robin Hood: Men in Tights

"Like everything which is not the involuntary result of fleeting emotion but the creation of time and will, any marriage, happy or unhappy, is infinitely more interesting than any romance, however passionate."

W.H. Auden

"Everyone should be married.
A bachelor's life is no life for a
single man."

Sam Goldwyn

"A married couple are well suited when
both partners usually feel the need for a
quarrel at the same time."

Jean Rostand

"A bridegroom is a man who has
spent a lot of money on a suit that
no one notices."

Josh Billings

Love and Marriage – Celebrity Style

"It is really rare to find someone you really, really love and that you want to spend your life with and all that stuff that goes along with being married. I am one of those lucky people. And I think she feels that way too. So the romantic stuff is easy because you want them to be happy."

Harry Connick, Jr.

"I'd imagine my wedding as a fairytale... huge, beautiful and white."

Paris Hilton

"If I get married, I want to
be very married."

Audrey Hepburn

"There's a big difference between
falling in love with someone and
falling in love with someone and
getting married. Usually, after you
get married, you fall in love with
the person even more."

Dave Grohl

"Getting married, for me, was the best thing I ever did. I was suddenly beset with an immense sense of release, that we have something more important than our separate selves, and that is the marriage. There's immense happiness that can come from working towards that."

Nick Cave

"I wouldn't be caught dead marrying a woman old enough to be my wife."

Tony Curtis

"I think if you're at the point where you're popular enough to sell your wedding photos to *OK! Magazine* then you don't need the money."

Johnny Vegas

"I know a lot of people didn't expect our relationship to last, but we've just celebrated our two months' anniversary."

Britt Ekland

"I proposed to Neil. It wasn't a question. It was an order."

Christine Hamilton

"A good friend just told me that the key to a successful marriage was to argue naked!"

LeAnn Rimes

"The ideal husband understands every word his wife doesn't say."

Alfred Hitchcock

"Marriage is about the most expensive way for the average man to get laundry done."

Burt Reynolds

"Sometimes I bust out and do things so permanent. Like tattoos and marriage."

Drew Barrymore

"For marriage to be a success, every woman and every man should have their own bathroom!"

Catharine Zeta-Jones

"I used to say to my dad how did you and mom stay married for all this time? And he'd say, 'Two things: number one you've got to have the same dreams... number two we never wanted to get divorced at the same time.'"

Gwynneth Paltrow

"Everybody needs love. There are a lot of guys you think are hard core gangsters, but all these guys' weaknesses are women. Look at the movie *Scarface*. At the end of the day he just wanted to have kids with his woman."

Master P

"You have to keep the fights clean and the sex dirty."

Kevin Bacon

"Women rule the world. It's not really worth fighting because they know what they are doing. Ask Napoleon, ask Adam, ask Richard Burton or Richie Sambora. Many a man has crumbled."

Jon Bon Jovi

"When you end up happily married even the failed relationships have worked beautifully to get you there."

Julia Roberts

"There's no bad consequence to loving fully with all your heart. You always gain by giving love."

Reece Witherspoon

"Before you marry a person, you should first make them use a computer with slow Internet to see who they really are."

Will Ferrell

"Love is absolute loyalty. People
fade, looks fade, but loyalty never fades.
You can depend so much on certain
people; you can set your watch by
them. And that's love, even if it
doesn't seem very exciting."

Sylvester Stallone

"I never take any commitment lightly
and I certainly don't take my wife
lightly. I never did and I never will.
That's permanent. That's true love."

John Lydon

"My bounty is as boundless as
the sea. My love is deep. The more
I give to thee the more I have.
For both are infinite."

Shakespeare, Romeo and Juliet

"I was and am swept away.
I believe in life there are some
things you can't deny or rationalize.
And this is one of them."

Cate Blanchett

"I believe in love at first sight – but it hasn't happened to me yet."

Leonardo DiCaprio

"We're born alone, we live alone, we die alone. Only through our love and friendship can we create the illusion for the moment that we're not alone."

Orson Welles

"Love, for me, is someone telling me, 'I want to be with you for the rest of my life, and if you needed me to, I'd jump out of a plane for you.'"

Jennifer Lopez

"I like to believe that love is a reciprocal thing. It can't be felt, truly, by one."

Sean Penn

"Don't marry unless you look at that person and say, 'I can't get out of bed in the morning knowing she's out there.'"

Alec Baldwin

"Men want the same thing from their underwear that they want from women: a little bit of support and a little bit of freedom."

Jerry Seinfeld

"Marriage is really tough, because
you have to deal with feelings
and lawyers."

Richard Pryor

"My mom's always bragging about
the dumbest stuff. The other day she
was telling me, she's like, 'You know I
can still fit in my wedding dress.' I was
like, 'Oh my god, who cares, right?'
I mean it is weird that she's the same
size now as she was when she was eight
months pregnant."

Amy Schumer

"Marry Prince William? I'd love that. Who wouldn't want to be a princess?"

Britney Spears

"It's important when you're married not to forget those things you used to do when you were trying to get her to marry you. You can't send flowers and buy gifts then, when you're married, say, 'Right, get my tea on.' That doesn't go down well. So you've got to keep that level of interest going."

David Walliams

"Before I met you, before I even knew you existed, I knew you were coming. I was ready to give my whole heart to someone and now here you are. Sometimes I think I'm going to explode from how much I love you. I'm completely consumed by you. And tonight, we get to become one. I promise to love you until after my heart bursts... You're my dream and my reality, my future and my present, my whole heart and my best friend."

Catherine Giudici's wedding vow to
Sean Lowe

"From the moment I met you, I wanted more. I wanted more of your infectious smile, I wanted more of your adorable giggle and I wanted more of your love. You had me hooked from the beginning."

Sean Lowe's wedding vow to Catherine Giudici

"I promise to always make his favourite banana milkshake."

Jennifer Aniston to Brad Pitt

"I promise to split the difference
on the thermostat."

Brad Pitt to Jennifer Aniston

"Selfishness has no place in a
lasting relationship. Happiness is
what each of you should seek for
the other. Ask less for yourself than
you are willing to give. Love can be
shown by a word or touch or two
thoughts entwined as one. In every
relationship, trust is very important;
never break that trust."

*From the wedding of
Michael Jordan and Juanita R. Vanoy*

"From this day forward I promise to be worth it. Worth the time. Worth the trip. Worth the energy. Worth the embarrassment. Worth your love. I promise that you will always count. You will always come first and, of course, if you don't for whatever reason, I will buy you some shoes."

John Caprulo's wedding vow

"The little things are the big things. It is never being too old to hold hands. It is remembering to say 'I love you' at least once a day. It is never going to sleep angry. It is at no time taking the other for granted; the courtship should not end with the honeymoon, it should continue through all the years. It is having a mutual sense of values and common objectives. It is standing together facing the world."

From the wedding of

Paul Newman and Joanne Woodward

More Words
of Wisdom

"A wedding is an event. Marriage is a lifetime. Invest more in your marriage than your wedding and success is inevitable."

Myles Munroe

"Never marry a man with a big head. Because you're going to give birth to that man's child and you want a baby with a narrow head."

Jilly Goolden

"My recipe for marital happiness is, whenever you can, read at meals."

Cyril Connolly

"Husbands and wives, first, be faithful to each other. Second, keep the romance going all of your life by courting each other every day."

Zig Ziglar

"My dad says finding somebody that when you are old is going to wipe your arse – that's marriage."

Jason Manford

"Some people ask the secret of our long marriage. We take time to go to a restaurant two times a week. A little candlelight, dinner, music and dancing. She goes Tuesdays. I go Fridays."

Henry Youngman

"I chose my wife, as she did her wedding gown, for qualities that would wear well."

Oliver Goldsmith

"Never cry over a man. Just yell 'Next!'"

Denise Gilbert

"To have a happy marriage, tell your spouse everything, except the essentials."

Cynthia Noble

"But let there be spaces in your togetherness and let the winds of the heavens dance between you. Love one another but make not a bond of love: let it rather be a moving sea between the shores of your souls."

Khalil Gibran

"It doesn't matter how often a couple have sex as long as it is the same number for both of them."

Marian Mills

"A successful marriage requires falling in love many times, always with the same person."

Mignon McLaughlin

"I have learned that only two things are necessary to keep one's wife happy. First, let her think she's having her own way. And second, let her have it."

Lyndon B. Johnson

"A happy marriage is the union
of two good forgivers."

Robert Quillen

"A good marriage is one which
allows for change and growth in
the individuals and in the way they
express their love."

Pearl S. Buck

"The greatest marriages are
built on teamwork. A mutual
respect, a healthy dose of
admiration, and a never-ending
portion of love and grace."

Fawn Weaver

"In a marriage, each partner is
to be an encourager rather than
a critic, a forgiver rather than a
collector of hurts, and an enabler
rather than a reformer."

Anon

"Coming together is a beginning;
keeping together is progress;
working together is success."

Henry Ford

"When the darkness rolls in, I'll be
there through thick and thin."

Hilary Duff

"The secret of a happy marriage
remains a secret."

Henny Youngman

"Experts on romance say for a happy marriage there has to be more than a passionate love. For a lasting union, they insist, there must be a genuine liking for each other. Which, in my book, is a good definition for friendship."

Marilyn Monroe

"Remember, we all stumble; every one of us. That is why it's a comfort to go hand in hand."

Emily Kimbrough

"Marriages, like a garden, take time to grow. But the harvest is rich unto those who patiently and tenderly care for the ground."

Darlene Schacht

"To keep your marriage brimming, with love in the wedding cup, whenever you're wrong, admit it; whenever you're right, shut up."

Ogden Nash

"If you have been married more than ten years, being good in bed means you don't steal the covers."

Brenda Davidson

"A perfect marriage is just two imperfect people who refuse to give up on each other."

Anon

"The ideal marriage consists of a deaf husband and a blind wife."

Paidraig Colum

"A marriage is not a noun; it's a verb. It isn't something you get. It's the way you love your partner every day."

Barbara de Angelis

"A great marriage is not when the 'perfect couple' comes together. It is when an imperfect couple learns to enjoy their differences."

Dave Muerer

"A good marriage is that in which each appoints the other guardian of his solitude."

Rainer Maria Rilke

"A happy marriage is a long conversation which always seems too short."

Andre Maurois

"Don't stop dating your wife and never stop flirting with your husband."

Anon

"What counts in making a happy marriage is not so much how compatible you are, but how you deal with incompatibility."

Leo Tolstoy

"Remember, marriage is a two-way street. I don't know what that means, but remember it."

George Burns

"Love is ideal. Marriage is real.
The confusion of the two shall
never go unpunished."

J.W. von Goethe

"The secret of a successful marriage
is not to be at home too much."

Colin Chapman

"Women like silent men. They think
they are listening."

Marcel Achard

"Never try to impress a woman,
because if you do she'll expect you
to keep up the standard for the rest
of your life. And the pace, my
friends, is devastating."

W.C. Fields

"After seven years of marriage,
I'm sure of just two things: first,
never wallpaper together, and
second, you'll need two bathrooms,
both for her."

Dennis Miller

"A wife is a person who can look in a drawer and find her husband's socks that aren't there."

Dan Bennett

"Everything my wife and I do is on a 50-50 basis – I tell her what to do and she tells me where to go."

Mitch Murray

"All men make mistakes, but married men find out about them sooner."

Red Skelton

"My husband always felt that a marriage and career don't mix. That's why he's never worked."

Phyllis Diller

"Marriage is a partnership – she finds the bugs and I have to kill them."

Scott King

"Every time you talk to your wife,
a voice in your head should say...
'This conversation will be recorded
for training and quality purposes.'"

Anon

"Love grows by giving. The love
we give away is the only love we
keep. The only way to retain
love is to give it away."

Elbert Hubbard

Together
Forever

"Our wedding was many
years ago. The celebration
continues to this day."

Gene Perret

"Being in a long marriage is a little
bit like that nice cup of coffee every
morning – I might have it every
day, but I still enjoy it."

Stephen Gaine

"Being someone's first love
may be great, but to be their last is
beyond perfect."

Anon

"What I really want to do with
my life – what I want to do for a
living – is be with your daughter.
I'm good at it."

Lloyd, Say Anything

"The half-life of love is forever."
Junot Diaz

"Whatever our souls are made of,
his and mine are the same."
Emily Brontë

"Grow old along with me;
the best is yet to be."
Robert Browning

"Love seems the swiftest, but it is the slowest of all growths. No man or woman really knows what perfect love is until they have been married a quarter of a century."

Mark Twain

"It is better to have loved even your wife than never to have loved at all."

Edgar Saltus

"I don't know where I'd be
without you here with me. Life with
you makes perfect sense.
You're my best friend."

Tim McGraw

"There is no such thing as a perfect
man or a perfect marriage. But the
one I have is perfect for me."

Fawn Weaver

"The beauty of marriage is
not always seen from the very
beginning... but rather as love grows
and develops over time."

Fawn Weaver

"Once upon a time there was a boy
who loved a girl, and her laughter
was a question he wanted to spend
his whole life answering."

Nicole Krauss

"In the arithmetic of love, one plus one equals everything, and two minus one equals nothing."

Mignon McLaughlin

"When my wife complained that I never told her I loved her, I said, 'I told you I loved you when we got married and if I ever change my mind, I'll let you know.'"

Liam O'Reilly

"Contrary to what many women believe it's easy to develop a long-term, intimate and mutually fulfilling relationship with a male. Of course, the male has to be a Labrador retriever."

Dave Berry

"But to sustain a marriage for 50 years, you have to get real a little bit and find someone who is understanding and who you can grow with. My mom always says, 'Marry the man who loves you a millimetre more.'"

Ali Larte

"We may have started as individuals, but now we are as one."

Bryon Pulsifer

"A lot of people like the idea of eternal love and eternal romance. The notion of love that is more profound and deeper, because it is eternal, is very powerful."

James Patterson

"Being deeply loved by someone gives you strength while loving someone deeply gives you courage."

Lao Tzu

"Happy is the man who finds a true friend, and far happier is he who finds that true friend in his wife."

Franz Schubert

"I love my husband very much.
I knew it was real true love because
I felt like I could be myself around
that person. Your true, true
innermost authentic self, the stuff
you don't let anyone else see, if you
can be that way with that person, I
think that thats real love."

Idina Menzel

"Affection is responsible for nine-
tenths of whatever solid and durable
happiness there is in our lives."

C.S. Lewis

"Because it is the nature of love to create, a marriage itself is something which has to be created, so that, together we become a new creature. To marry is the biggest risk in human relations that a person can take."

Madeleine L'Engle

"There is no more lovely, friendly and charming relationship, communion or company than a good marriage."

Martin Luther

"I've chosen my wedding ring large and heavy to continue forever. But exactly because of that all the time that Dave and I have an argument I feel it like handcuffs, and on anger time I throw it in a basket. Poor Dave, he bought me three wedding rings already!"

Carmen Miranda

"You're mine. Mine, as I'm yours. And if we die, we die. All men must die, Jon Snow. But first, we'll live."

Game of Thrones

"For years my wedding ring has done its job. It has led me not into temptation. It has reminded my husband numerous times at parties that it's time to go home. It has been a source of relief to a dinner companion. It has been a status symbol in the maternity ward."

Erma Bombeck

"We get old and get used to each other. We think alike. We read each others minds. We know what the other wants without asking. Sometimes we irritate each other a little bit. Maybe sometimes take each other for granted. But once in awhile, like today, I meditate on it and realise how lucky I am to share my life with the greatest woman I ever met."

Johnny Cash